TOLULADE FOLARIN

FROM A BROKEN HOME

FROM A BROKEN HOME

Understanding love, healing the wounds of broken homes, and building healthier relationships

by
Tolulade Folarin (Nee Otayemi)

Featuring writings from
Hector Otayemi
Adeyinka Otayemi
Ololade Otayemi
Oluwademilade Otayemi

(True life story of Hector Otayemi family)

ISBN 978-1-997604-36-5

About the Book: From a Broken Home

From a Broken Home is a deeply personal and heartfelt journey through the pain, confusion, and eventual healing that follows when the foundation of family is shaken. Written with honesty and compassion, this book explores the lasting impact of growing up in a home fractured by separation or divorce and the powerful truth that one's past does not have to dictate one's future.

Drawing from her own story and the experiences of others, the author shares reflections on the emotional, spiritual, and relational consequences of a broken home.

Each chapter takes readers through real-life moments of struggle, discovery, and growth, offering comfort to those who have lived through similar pain. More importantly, it provides hope, showing that beauty can rise from brokenness.

This book is for anyone who has ever wondered if their background disqualifies them from experiencing a healthy, loving relationship or building a strong family of their own. It is for those carrying invisible scars from their parents' conflicts, as well as for those currently navigating challenges in their own marriages. Through storytelling, practical wisdom, and faith-based encouragement, *From a Broken Home* reminds readers that healing is possible, that cycles can be broken, and that God can write a new story from even the most painful beginnings.

Each page is an invitation to look beyond the hurt and see the hand of restoration at work, to believe again in love, in family, and in the possibility of wholeness. Because no matter how broken the past may be, the future can still be beautiful.

Prologue

Why This Story Matters:

Some stories are difficult to tell but even harder to keep silent. *From a Broken Home* is one of those stories. It's about my journey through the aftermath of my parents' separation- a journey marked by heartache, confusion, resilience, and ultimately, redemption. But this book is not just about me. It's for anyone who has lived through the pain of a fractured family, who has felt the ripple effects of broken relationships, or who longs to create a healthier and stronger foundation for themselves and future generations.

Growing up in the shadow of my parents' broken marriage, I often found myself grappling with questions I couldn't answer: *Why did this happen? Could it have been prevented? Am I destined to repeat the same mistakes?* These questions haunted me, but they also drove me to seek understanding and healing. Along the way, I discovered that I was not alone in my struggles. Many others have walked this path, and many more are still navigating it.

This book is my way of reaching out to you. Whether you are a child of separation, someone grappling with the effects of your parents' choices, an unmarried person seeking to build a strong foundation for marriage, or a couple struggling to mend what feels broken beyond repair, my hope is that these pages will bring you hope, clarity, and guidance. I've come to learn that the pain of a broken home doesn't have to define us. While it shapes us, it can also be the catalyst for growth, wisdom, and transformation. Through my own experiences, as well as the stories of others who have faced similar challenges, I'll share lessons learned, mistakes made, and practical tools for healing and building stronger relationships. Above all, this book is about redemption-the kind of redemption that turns pain into purpose and brokenness into beauty. It's about finding strength in vulnerability and hope in the most unlikely places.

So, let's take this journey together. Let's explore what it means to rise from the ashes of brokenness, to forgive, to heal, and to create a brighter future. No matter where you're starting from, know that there is a path forward. There is hope. And there is a way to turn the story of *From a Broken Home* into one of healing, love, and restoration.

This would be my most vulnerable project yet because it exposes a lot, not just about me but about others, some of those who mean a lot to me. My prayer for you is that you are liberated and enlightened through the content of the book. Oh, pardon me. I am yet to introduce myself. Hello dear reader, my name is Tolulade, you can call me Tolu. Here is the tale of my parents' broken marriage. What did it make of me? And what is your business with it? Relax and enjoy reading.

Tolu Folarin

CHAPTER 1 - THE FIRST CRY

I remember the first time I ever saw my mum cry was in the year 2005. This was the year that my paternal grandfather was buried and I was in primary 3 - this would be equivalent to grade 1. I still remember the scenarios, not vividly but in flashes. The remembrance is because I found it weird to see mummy cry- a whole superwoman, as I thought of her to be. I never knew the real reason why she cried until years after. I knew there were issues between her and my dad but I never knew what exactly those issues were. So, I initially assumed that she cried because someone died. Afterall, we were preparing for my paternal grandpa's funeral.

My grandpa had died in December and was set to be buried in February. Prior to this time, I never really knew my dad, I only remembered seeing him a few times and I was not really bothered because my mom would always say he traveled and my brothers never said otherwise. So, when I heard that we were going to see him at my grandpa's funeral, I was so excited. Mind you, I never really knew my grandpa, I was told that we met a couple of times when I was younger, and I recall meeting him a few times at my uncle's house while he was sick before his demise. I never really got to know him because my parents' marriage started to go south before I was

born. So, there were some strained family relationships.
My initial assumption when I saw my super mom cry did not last long after I looked closely and saw that she was on the floor kneeling, while the others (mostly men) seated under the tent were seated on the chair. One of them leaned forward and held her shoulders. TO BE CONTINUED…

BOOK LAUNCH ON MAY 22, 2026

https://linktr.ee/TOLULADEFOLARIN

www.tolufolarin.ca

CHAPTER 2 - LOVERS UNTIL DEATH

As a teenager watching my parents' relationship unravel, I began to question everything I thought I knew about love, trust, and commitment. If two people who loved each other so fiercely couldn't make it work, what hope was there for me? What guarantee did marriage offer, really? These questions quietly followed me into my young adulthood, shaping my thoughts and decisions in ways I didn't immediately recognize.

TO BE CONTINUED…

BOOK LAUNCH ON MAY 22, 2026

https://linktr.ee/TOLULADEFOLARIN

www.tolufolarin.ca

Looking back now, I realize that the end of my parents' marriage wasn't just their story; it became a defining part of mine. It shaped how I saw the world, how I approached relationships, and how I understood myself. This chapter of my life was painful, but it also marked the beginning of a journey toward understanding, healing, and ultimately, hope. In the chapters ahead, I'll share more about that journey, as well as the lessons I've learned along the way. But for now, I want to pause and acknowledge the reality of this moment. For anyone who has experienced the breaking of their family's foundation, know that you are not alone. The pain is real, but so is the possibility of healing. When the walls fall down, it can feel like the end of everything. But sometimes, it's also the beginning of something new. As hard as it was to see at the time, that's exactly what it was for me. And it can be for you, too.

TO BE CONTINUED…

BOOK LAUNCH ON MAY 22, 2026

https://linktr.ee/TOLULADEFOLARIN

www.tolufolarin.ca

Step-by-Step Process of Conflict Resolution for Parents and Children

Every family faces conflict, but when a marriage breaks, the ripple effects can feel endless. Parents grieve the loss of what was; children wrestle with what will never be the same. Yet even in brokenness, God is present - rebuilding, restoring, and renewing what we thought was lost. This chapter offers faith-based, step-by-step processes for parents seeking peace and children pursuing healing, whether they desire marriage or not.

When parents learn to manage conflict differently, the whole family benefits. When children learn to heal, they can make empowered choices whether they choose marriage or a different path. This chapter gives clear, compassionate, step-by-step processes for both parents and children. Use these as practical guides, not rigid rules. Healing and reconciliation are messy; these steps simply help you move with intention.

Conflict in marriage is normal; unresolved conflict is what damages families. The goal of conflict resolution is not to be right but to be connected, to repair, and to model healthy relationship skills for children.Broken marriages often carry layers of hurt, misunderstanding, and disappointment. But with humility and grace, healing and peace are still possible, even if reconciliation doesn't mean reunion.

"If it is possible, as far as it depends on you, live at peace with everyone." - Romans 12:18

Before you begin: Prepare the ground

1. **Choose the right time and place.** No urgent talks in the heat of the moment or when tired; pick neutral space and an agreed time.

2. **Set the intention.** State quietly: "I want to understand and repair this." Make the shared goal the relationship, not victory.
3. **Agree on rules.** No name-calling, no walking out without a plan, no bringing children into the middle.

TO BE CONTINUED…

BOOK LAUNCH ON MAY 22, 2026

https://linktr.ee/TOLULADEFOLARIN

www.tolufolarin.ca

TOLULADE FOLARIN

www.ingramcontent.com/pod-product-compliance
Lightning Source LLC
LaVergne TN
LVHW010842120826
845149LV00020B/3492